WASHINGTON, D.C.

FROM ABOVE

CAMERON DAVIDSON

Text by
MAGDA NAKASSIS

MYRIAD BOOKS

WHEN THE NATION was born in 1776, the need for a capital city arose. Before George Washington settled upon 10 square miles on the Potomac River, the country had eight different capitals – and Congress desperately needed a place to call home. In 1791, engineer Pierre Charles L'Enfant drew up plans for an awe-inspiring city, a network of grand circles radiating into wide, tree-lined boulevards. Looking at the wild swampland that Washington had selected, it would have been nearly impossible to envisage L'Enfant's perfectly planned city: Washington, D.C. as it stands today. As the nation's capital, Washington, D.C. inspires a sense of power and grandeur – from its monumental government buildings to the gleaming white marble of its presidential memorials. Its architecture is laden with symbolism, and physical aspects of the capital are designed to represent ideas of freedom and democracy. L'Enfant ensured that the home of the President, Congress and the Supreme Court would be a beautiful city, its tremendous buildings balanced by wild parks and natural beauty.

▲ THE CAPITAL BELTWAY was christened the "road of opportunity" when its ribbon was cut in 1964. With eight lanes of traffic, 40 interchanges and 64 miles of road, the Beltway handles as many as 225,000 commuters every day.

▶ THE UNITED STATES CAPITOL is the most powerful and symbolic building in Washington, D.C. Positioned at the exact center of the city, the Capitol building is the heart of the legislative branch of the federal government, and the original home of Congress. It has come to embody the nation's tenets of freedom, liberty and justice. Construction began in 1793, and over the years the Capitol has been burnt, rebuilt, extended and restored – a testament to the endurance of the American people and their government. Crowning the magnificent cast-iron dome is the Statue of Freedom, a classical female figure. Designed and built by sculptor Thomas Crawford, Freedom holds a laurel wreath of victory, standing 19ft 6in tall and weighing 7.5 tons. By an Act of Congress, no building in D.C. can exceed 15 stories, ensuring that the Capitol Building is the tallest – and that nothing stands above Freedom.

The **LIBRARY OF CONGRESS** is the world's largest library and home to over 126 million books, recordings, photographs, manuscripts, etc. The archive grew out of the personal collection of Thomas Jefferson (1743-1826), who believed that the continual pursuit of truth and knowledge was essential for a free government.

UNION STATION stands 96ft high and sprawls over 200 acres of land, embodying the capital's monumental character. When it was built in 1907, it became the largest train station in the world – and cost an unprecedented $125 million! Its architect, Daniel Burnham, modeled the building's façade on the Arch of Constantine in Rome, thereby setting a pattern for neoclassical architecture throughout the city.

◄ DEDICATED TO THE "Father of his Country", the **WASHINGTON MONUMENT** towers above the city, standing 600 ft tall. The simple but imposing obelisk offers an incredible view – you can take an elevator to the top.

▲ A BIRD'S EYE VIEW from the top of the Washington Monument sees 1600 Pennsylvania Avenue, America's most familiar address. A must-see for both tourists and natives alike, the **WHITE HOUSE** is the

President's private residence, and an important symbol of the United States government and its people. The White House has been the home of every president since John Adams, and has survived two fires – including one ignited by the British during the War of 1812. Externally, the White House's better-known side faces the South Lawn, a favorite site for presidential speeches. On the south side, the grounds are buffered by a patch of green called The Ellipse, and to the north is Lafayette Park.

▲ THE MALL IS lined with the **SMITHSONIAN INSTITUTION** buildings, whose impressive collection of some 143 million artworks and specimens is housed in museums dedicated to art, history and science. This massive project was funded by James Smithson, a scientist who, in 1935, bequeathed his estate to the USA. The most popular of all 16 museums is the National Air and Space Museum, whose modern glass and pink marble design sets it apart. Visitors flock from around the globe to see the Wright Brothers' 1903 flyer, touch a chunk of lunar rock and taste the freeze-dried ice cream that NASA astronauts eat in space. Beyond stands the Smithsonian Institution Building, nicknamed "the Castle" for its 12th-century Norman-style architecture, built of red sandstone. In the distance stands the **LINCOLN MEMORIAL**, a replica of a Greek temple that faces the rectangular reflecting pool.

▶ FACING SOUTH, a snowy view of the city center reveals the proximity of the White House, the towering Washington Monument and the Jefferson Memorial.

◀ NAMED AFTER Civil War hero Samuel Francis duPont, **DUPONT CIRCLE** is one of the city's most vibrant and stylish neighborhoods. The area was a wild marshland until the 1870s, when a group of senators and wealthy businessmen made it their home. Today it is chock full of boutiques, cafés, street performers, art galleries and diplomatic embassies – conveniently lodged between downtown D.C. and the greenery of Rock Creek Park.

▲ TRAVELING SOUTH, you come to the imposing **JEFFERSON MEMORIAL**, which sits on the edge of the Potomac River, overlooking the Tidal Basin. In 1939 Franklin D. Roosevelt laid the cornerstone for a memorial dedicated to Thomas Jefferson, founding father of the

United States and the country's third president. Within that cornerstone is a copy of the Declaration of Independence and the Constitution, two of Jefferson's greatest achievements. The monument was designed to resemble the Pantheon of Rome, which Jefferson considered the perfect example of a circular building. When designing his own home, Monticello, and the "academical village" he founded, the University of Virginia, the Pantheon was his own inspiration. Within the marble colonnade is a larger-than-life bronze statue of Thomas Jefferson, along with several inscriptions. Each engraving quotes Jefferson's writings, from letters to George Washington and James Madison, to A Bill for Establishing Religious Freedom.

◀ **THE THEODORE ROOSEVELT BRIDGE** spans the Potomac River, linking Virginia to the nation's capital. The bridge crosses the tip of the **THEODORE ROOSEVELT ISLAND PARK** (below), a 91-acre forest that commemorates the 26th president and his love of the great outdoors. On the banks of the Potomac River is the white and gold **JOHN F. KENNEDY CENTER FOR THE PERFORMING ARTS**, a "living memorial" to JFK and the heart of music, dance and theater in Washington. To its left is **THE WATERGATE HOTEL**, which saw the most notorious political scandal in American history.

▼ RUNNING ALONGSIDE the Potomac is the **CHESAPEAKE & OHIO CANAL**, originally used to haul coal into the city. Though the canal has fallen into disuse, its towpath is now a nature trail offering spectacular views of the Potomac River Valley.

▲ **GEORGETOWN** began as an 18th-century tobacco trading port, named in honor of King George II. The town quickly grew prosperous, and was incorporated into Washington, D.C. in 1871. But at the turn of the century, Georgetown suffered a severe economic depression, transforming the once-fashionable quarter into a slum. Now, Georgetown is one of the most prestigious and charming neighborhoods in the city, with its well-preserved Victorian townhouses, cobblestone streets and famous historic district.

▶ SEATED ATOP A steep hill is **GEORGETOWN UNIVERSITY**, one of the most distinguished institutions for research and education, as well as the nation's oldest Catholic university.

AT DUSK, gleaming headlights show the traffic flowing in and out of the city, across the Theodore Roosevelt, Arlington Memorial and 14th Street bridges.

▲ TRAVELING NORTH on the Potomac River, you reach **WASHINGTON HARBOR**, a modern complex of offices, retail shops, restaurants and luxury condominiums. Situated in trendy Georgetown, with a boardwalk overlooking the Potomac River, its waterfront condos can sell for millions of dollars.

◄ THE BUSTLING harbor of Alexandria, Virginia has seen everything – from its colonial days trading flour and hemp to the battles of the Revolutionary and Civil Wars. Today, Alexandria boasts an array of cultural and historic institutions.

ARLINGTON NATIONAL CEMETERY (right) is the burial ground for more than a quarter of a million of the nation's best and brightest – including war heroes, explorers, presidents and Supreme Court justices. In 1920, **THE MEMORIAL AMPHITHEATER AT ARLINGTON NATIONAL CEMETERY** (above) was dedicated to every American who died serving his country. Inscribed on its stage are Lincoln's words from the Gettysburg Address: "We here highly resolve that these dead shall not have died in vain." One of the most visited graves is President Kennedy's (left), where Jacqueline Kennedy lit an eternal flame in his memory.

◀ WASHINGTON, D.C. has many houses of worship. The **WASHINGTON NATIONAL CATHEDRAL** is a delayed response to George Washington's appeal for a non-denominational national church, open to all. Although the foundation stone was laid in 1907, construction was not completed until 1990, making it the world's youngest Gothic structure.

▲ **THE TEMPLE OF THE CHURCH OF JESUS CHRIST OF LATTER-DAY SAINTS** has 175,000 members, and its six remarkable spires soar above the Capital Beltway. **THE BASILICA OF THE NATIONAL SHRINE OF THE IMMACULATE CONCEPTION** (above right), is on the campus of the Catholic University of America.

▶ IN HONOR of America's most eminent Freemason, the **GEORGE WASHINGTON MASONIC NATIONAL MEMORIAL** celebrates civic and religious liberty.

THE COLOSSAL, ultramodern **FEDEX FIELD** was built in 1997. Home of the Washington Redskins football team, the stadium contains 80,116 seats, four scoreboards and two huge video screens for replays and announcements.

ON THE outskirts of the city, the Women's Soccer Team for the Catholic University of America – also known as the Fighting Cardinals – run the field outside the **RAYMOND A. DUFOUR ATHLETIC CENTER**.

IN THE inner city, children romp around the **KENNEDY PLAYGROUND**, where basketball courts, a skate park and a rec center have replaced a local junkyard.

HALYCON HOUSE, situated in historic Georgetown, was built by the first Secretary of the Navy in 1783. The Georgian house is said to be haunted by its original owner, and attracts many curious visitors – including "ghost hunters."

◀ **MOUNT VERNON**, George Washington's private home, lies south of the capital, deep in the heart of Virginia. Every year, over a million visitors come to view his beautiful mansion, which overlooks the Maryland shoreline across the Potomac River, and the estate, with its country lanes, serpentine trails and manicured gardens.

▼ THE GREENERY of the **NATIONAL ZOOLOGICAL PARK** is a lovely contrast to the concrete jungle that surrounds it. As diplomats and senators carry on with their day to day business, flamingos, giant pandas, Sumatran tigers and a family of western lowland gorillas roam 163 acres of urban park in the city center.

ONLY 10 minutes from the Capitol Building is **THE UNITED STATES NATIONAL ARBORETUM**, a vast green area that is Washington, D.C.'s best kept secret. Here 446 acres of land have been landscaped to showcase its collections and gardens – including bonsai trees, a wild valley full of prairie plants and an aquatic garden teeming with Japanese cart fish, water lilies and cattails. Standing tall on a knoll in the Ellipse Meadow are the **NATIONAL CAPITOL COLUMNS**. The columns originally belonged to the East Portico of the Capitol Building, but when its massive cast-iron dome was assembled larger than planned and weighing roughly 4.5 tons, the delicate sandstone Corinthian columns had to be removed. A place was found for them in the arboretum, where they could command 20 empty acres of meadowland. The columns overlook a small reflecting pool, making it a picturesque spot for wedding photography.

First published in 2004 by Myriad Books Limited
35 Bishopsthorpe Road, London SE26 4PA

Photographs copyright © Cameron Davidson
Text copyright © Magda Nakassis

ISBN 0 681642 62 9

Designed by Jerry Goldie

Printed in China